MIGRATION

JOURNEYS THROUGH
BLACK BRITISH HISTORY

We are so thrilled that you are reading The Black Curriculum's first books! It means so much to us as a team, and I hope that these books inspire you to dive into your passions, hopes, and dreams. Go be great!

LAVINYA STENNETT, FOUNDER AND CEO OF THE BLACK CURRICULUM

The Black Curriculum is an organisation dedicated to promoting the learning of Black British history in and out of schools.

THE BLACK CURRICULUM

MIGRATION

JOURNEYS THROUGH BLACK BRITISH HISTORY

WRITTEN BY
MILLIE MENSAH

ILLUSTRATED BY
CAMILLA RU

Contents

Black Loyalist
(Page 48)

John Blanke
(Page 37)

CHAPTER 1: ROMAN BRITAIN

CHAPTER 2: BRITAIN'S BLACK TUDORS

CHAPTER 3: MIGRATION IN THE 18TH AND 19TH CENTURIES

CHAPTER 4: MIGRATION AND THE "MOTHER COUNTRY"

The Beachy Head Lady (Page 22) →

Timeline

In this book, you will read all about amazing people and their stories. Here are some key dates placed in chronological order to help show when everything happened in history.

**BEACHY HEAD LADY
125-245 CE**
It is thought that she lived sometime between these dates.

125   **193**   **208**

EMPEROR LUCIUS SEPTIMIUS SEVERUS
becomes Emperor of Rome.

Septimius Severus and his army travel to Hadrian's Wall.

Britain is most involved with the Transatlantic Slave Trade between 1640 and 1807.

Fleet of ships sets sail for Sierra Leone settlement.

Committee for the Relief of the Black Poor founded.

1787 1786   **1783**   **1772**   **1640**

The British lose American War of Independence.

The case of James Somerset is brought to court.

Enslavement is officially made illegal by Parliament within the British Empire.

Empire Windrush docks at Tilbury Bay.

NHS founded.

1833   **1945**   **1948**

Mass migration of British nationals to Australia, New Zealand, and Canada **1945-1956**.

Parliament passes the British Nationality Act, so Commonwealth citizens can settle in Britain.

IPSWICH MAN comes to England **1258-1300**.

Catherine of Aragon arrives in England from Spain.

1258

1501

1511

JOHN BLANKE is a trumpeter at the royal procession around this time.

SIR FRANCIS DRAKE goes on final voyage to Caribbean.

1595

1588

1548

1545

Start of the Spanish Armada.

JACQUES FRANCIS gives evidence in court against his employer.

The *Mary Rose* ship sinks.

London Transport recruits employees from Jamaica and Barbados.

1953

1956

1966

Royal Coronation of Queen Elizabeth II.

London Transport recruits employees in Trinidad.

Foreword
by Oghenemaro Itoje

My name is Oghenemaro Itoje. I am a second-generation Nigerian British individual who has had the luxury of living between two strong and proud cultures. I use the word "luxury" on purpose, as I feel blessed that I can strongly identify with two proud but very distinct cultures. I love the duality that this lived experience gives me. I tell people that my parents raised me and my siblings in a very Nigerian household, in terms of culture, food, mindset, and behaviours. However, as soon as I stepped outside the front door I was in London, which was an environment that had different cultural norms and accepted behaviours. The African diaspora lived experience is different to other experiences; you have to find your place between the country of your birth and the country of your ancestry. This duality has been called "hyphenated identities". My parents spent a large proportion of their early life between Nigeria and the UK, partly for school, and partly for recreational time. They settled in the UK permanently in the early 90s after they married and decided to start their family in London. As a result, myself, my brother, and my sister came to the world with our new hyphenated identities.

Migration has been a vehicle that has propelled humanity forward. Migration is not a new concept, and one could argue it is a part of human nature. Since the dawn of humanity, we have been migrating from one place to another, learning from one another, and using that knowledge to make our societies better (for the most part). Science tells us that roughly two million years ago the earliest form of Homo erectus (upright humans) began its expansion from Africa, and since this time humans have been migrating from one place to another for all kinds of reasons. Modern technology has made migrating even easier and much more accessible to a wider proportion of society.

One cannot accurately tell the story of Britain without talking about the impact of migration. It is hard to think what modern-day Britain would look like without migration. The effects of migration are present in every facet of British life, whether it is our politics, our music, our health system, sport, business, media, and the list goes on. It is without question that migration has increased economic output and living standards within this society. Migration is an integral part of history and therefore Black history.

Through my passion for African art, and my understanding of the undeniable benefits of education to society, I have tried to challenge the narrative that Black history is a narrow segment of our lives and education. When referring to Black history, we tend to restrict it to three or four historical events mainly centred around the Transatlantic Slave Trade, American civil rights, and colonialism. While these events are important, they do not fully encapsulate the rich breadth of nuanced history that falls under Black history. When talking about history, we must try to portray the most accurate reflection of the past. Understanding migration and its effects is an important aspect of that.

Introduction

What is migration?

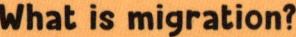

You probably know someone who wasn't born in this country but calls it home (or an additional home). Many of us who were born here have parents, grandparents, even great-grandparents who migrated to Britain. The TV and media might give us the impression that Black people's migration history is all about enslavement, or being invited over by the British government after World War II. These are important chapters in history, but they are not the full story.

So what is migration? A very simple meaning is "the movement of people from one area to another". An example would be someone moving from Canada to Australia or from Nigeria to the United States.

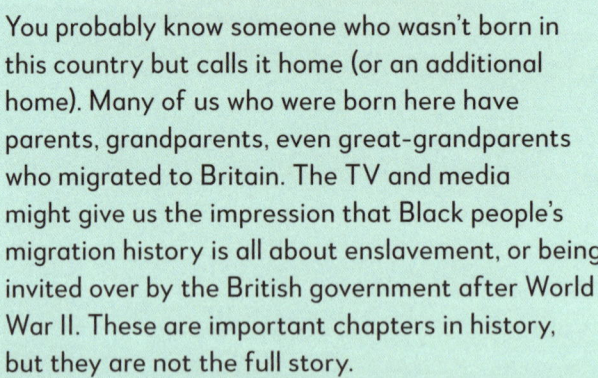

THE SPACIOUS COMFORTABLE LUXURIOUS
Santa Maria
SAILS **AUGUST 26**th
via VIGO SPAIN

BOOK NOW FOR **ENGLAND**
KINGSTON TO LONDON
FOR ONLY
£75

SEE YOUR TRAVEL AGENT IMMEDIATELY!
H. MACAULAY ORRETT LTD, 507 KING ST. KINGSTON

It is important to know that migration is not something that only just started happening recently. People have been doing it for thousands of years. It is also important that we look at all the ways Black people migrated to Britain; we need to understand that Black people's history is not only about enslavement. By looking deeper at Black people's migration stories, we gain a better understanding of their experiences.

What will be covered in this book?

Some of the earliest examples of migration from Africa began with the Roman era, with many people from North Africa settling in Roman Britain. There is concrete evidence that Africans lived in Britain way before Britain colonised certain countries as part of its empire. Africans moved freely, and some were held in high esteem in society. Spain and Portugal also played a role in Black people's migration to Britain. Tudor society acknowledged Black people as citizens, with many working as domestic servants, traders, musicians, and tailors.

Even though it is a difficult topic, we can't ignore the impact of enslavement on Black people. It is also important to look at how free Black people were treated during that time, and the Black people who were involved in the abolishment of slavery.

The final section of this book will look at the impact of migration to Britain after World War II and the ways Black people were encouraged by the British government to work and settle in Britain.

Roman Britain

We're going to start our journey in Roman Britain. From 43 CE to 410 CE, Britain was part of the Roman Empire. The Roman Empire spread across areas all around the Mediterranean Sea and further, including places in North Africa. People moved around within the empire, and some made the journey from North Africa to Britain.

Roman Britain

You might think that migration is something that started happening recently. But as far back as Roman times, people have been migrating to Britain from different places, including Africa.

So how do we know that African people lived in Roman Britain?

Scientists have used methods such as isotope analysis to find out where people came from.

Scientific methods have proved that some old skeletons from Roman Britain belonged to people of African descent. Isotope analysis is a remarkable method that has helped scientists identify the type of food and water people consumed. This helps to explore key differences in diets between migrants and the locals and can point to where certain skeletons originally came from. Using this science, we can find evidence of Africans in Roman Britain, giving us a clearer picture of migration in Roman Britain.

Septimius Severus and Hadrian's Wall

Hadrian's Wall is located on the border between present-day England and Scotland. This was the most northern region of the Roman Empire. When Britain was part of the Roman Empire, an African emperor called Emperor Lucius Septimius Severus came to live here. He was born in Leptis Magna, Libya, North Africa. The Romans wanted to conquer Scotland, so Emperor Lucius Septimius Severus brought with him the largest army (50,000 men) in the history of Roman Britain. They set up camp at Hadrian's Wall.

Septimius Severus would not have been the only African person of high ranking in the Roman military at this time. Eight other African men were also high up in the military within the northern Roman regiments. There were also African equestrian officers, as well as foot soldiers, in the Roman military. This means there was a community of Roman soldiers living by Hadrian's Wall, many of whom were African – **including the emperor himself!**

Septimius Severus

Looking at the Evidence

As well as isotope analysis, there are other things that tell us that Africans lived in Roman Britain.

The Aurelian Moors

An important piece of evidence was found in the village of Beaumont, towards the western end of Hadrian's Wall. Archaeologists found an altar stone with writing carved into it, dedicating it to the Roman god Jupiter. The writing also refers to the "Aurelian Moors". The Aurelian Moors were a military unit of North Africans named after the Emperor Marcus Aurelius.

The inscribed altar stone was found by archaeologists in 1934.

Another piece of evidence is the "Notitia Dignitatum". This document showed the details of the Roman Empire's military and civilian life. Surviving copies have shown evidence of a North African presence at Aballava, a fort on Hadrian's Wall. A section of the document refers to "the Aurelian Moors at Aballava".

A painting of Septimius Severus with his wife, Julia Domna, and his sons, Caracalla and Geta, still survives today.

Evidence like this shows that there were African soldiers living in Roman Britain. Some soldiers would have stayed in the area and raised families. These North African soldiers are an integral part of British history.

The Ivory Bangle Lady

In 1901, a skeleton was discovered in York. The skeleton became known as the Ivory Bangle Lady. She is proof that people came from Africa to Britain in Roman times.

The skeleton was discovered in a stone sarcophagus buried near an ordinary street in York. Scientific analysis showed that this person was female and had North African heritage. A Christian inscription was found with her: "Hail sister, may you live in God". This means she was likely a Christian when she died, which would mean that she belonged to a parish in Britain and was part of the local community.

White ivory bangle

Blue glass beaded necklace

Damaged bangle

Blue glass bottle, possibly once filled with perfumed oil

Black jet stone bangle

Yellow glass earrings

Glass disc may have been used as a mirror

She became known as the Ivory Bangle Lady, because she was buried with luxury goods including two bangles. One bangle was made from jet stone from Whitby, on the north east coast of England. The other was made from African ivory.

We might see her bangles as a powerful symbol of two cultures blending together. The bangles also hint at her high social status. Using isotope analysis, scientists could tell that she ate the same diet a lady of high status would have eaten.

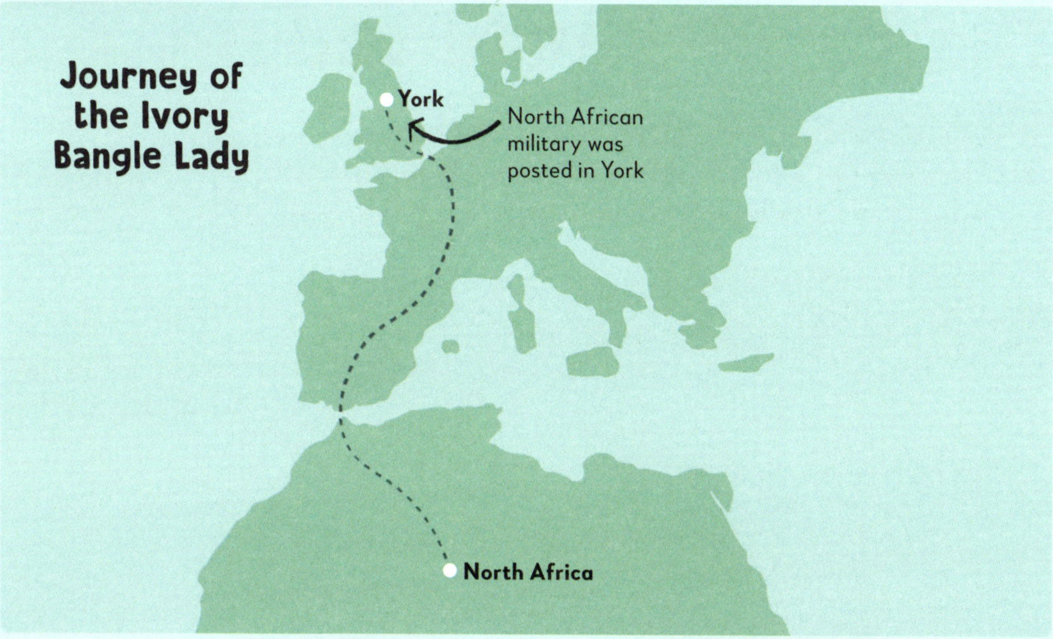

Journey of the Ivory Bangle Lady

York

North African military was posted in York

North Africa

How had she found herself in the north of England?

It was likely she had accompanied her family there when the North African military was posted in York. The discovery of the Ivory Bangle Lady tells us that women and children migrated across the Roman Empire as well as men. She is also an example of someone of African heritage who had high social status in Britain,

Ivory Bangle Lady

The Beachy Head Lady

Near the cliffs of Beachy Head on the south coast, another skeleton belonging to a female was discovered. She was named the Beachy Head Lady.

Where was the Beachy Head Lady from?

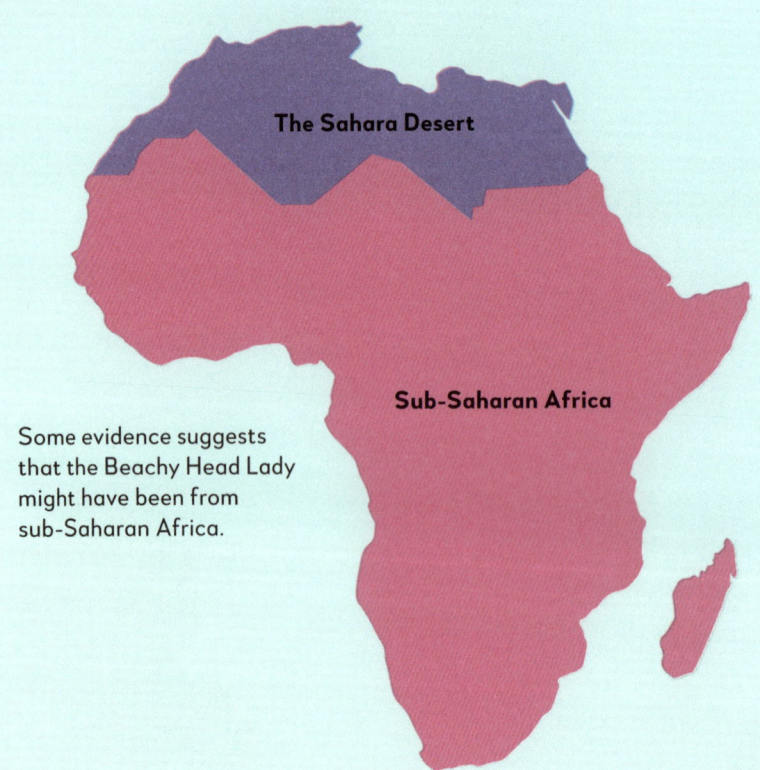

The Sahara Desert

Sub-Saharan Africa

Some evidence suggests that the Beachy Head Lady might have been from sub-Saharan Africa.

Isotope investigations indicate that she had a rich diet, much like the Ivory Bangle Lady, meaning she had a high social status. Some evidence suggests she might have been born in sub-Saharan Africa (which refers to African countries that are fully or partially south of the Sahara Desert). There is some debate, with some scientists believing she may have been from Cyprus. She lived sometime between 125 and 245 CE.

The Roman Empire didn't extend to the sub-Saharan region of Africa. If that is where she is from, it is interesting that she ended up on English shores. We might not know the reason she came to be in Britain, but the Beachy Head Lady might indicate that Africans from outside of the Roman Empire also made Britain their home.

Scientists have been able to reconstruct what the Beachy Head Lady might have looked like.

The Ipswich Man

Less than 30 years ago, archaeologists found another skeleton after digging in a monastery (a place where monks live) in Ipswich. This skeleton became known as the Ipswich Man.

Scientists confirmed that he was buried there between 1258 and 1300. So, he lived much later than the Ivory Bangle Lady and the Beachy Head Lady, but he is an important example of someone of African heritage living in pre-colonial Britain.

Archaeologists discovered the skeleton of the Ipswich Man on a dig.

Who was the Ipswich Man?

The Ipswich Man was from Tunis, Tunisia, in North Africa. How did he arrive in Britain? Records stated that four men, referred to as "Saracens", were brought back from the Crusades (a series of religious wars) by two men, Robert Tiptoft and Richard de Clare. Robert Tiptoft built the monastery. The Ipswich Man is thought to be one of the four men who came to Britain with him.

Saracens is a term Christians gave to Muslim people of Arab, Persian, and Turkish heritage.

The Ipswich Man likely lived in the monastery with the monks.

The Ipswich Man's connection to Christianity is relevant too. He most likely lived in the monastery with the monks, which means he was a valued member of the wider community. Investigations of his body show he died of an infection on his spine. It is likely he would have been looked after by the monks before he died. He was buried in the grounds of the monastery, and it would have been a Christian burial. So, much like the Ivory Bangle Lady, the Ipswich Man was a Christian when he died. Their religion is interesting because it means they were part of a community – their local parish. The Ivory Bangle Lady and the Ipswich Man both tell us that not only were there African people living in pre-colonial Britain, but that they were also rich and important figures in their communities.

How Was This Period of Time Positive for Africans?

The discovery of the Ipswich Man, Beachy Head Lady, and Ivory Bangle Lady highlighted how diverse England was, long before colonisation and the British Empire. Isotope analysis and forensic investigations have given us solid evidence of migration from Africa to England in pre-colonial times. We may not know everything about their stories, but we understand that migration is a big part of them.

What is race?

Race, as we know it today, is a category from the period of the Transatlantic Slave Trade. Race was used to justify the enslavement of Africans by colonisers. Race is based on appearance and where someone's ancestors are from. Race has not always existed throughout history, but is something that society has invented over time.

We've seen so far in this book that parts of England were more ethnically diverse in the past than we might have expected. There were lots of different groups of people living in Roman Britain, some of whom would have been Black. But the idea of "race" as something that was used to make horrible judgements about people and take away their resources didn't exist during Roman times.

That's not to say the Roman Empire was perfect – there was of course disease, enslavement, and robbery. Some people were certainly treated badly, but it would have been more because of their class and where they came from rather than their skin colour. People coming together under Roman citizenship can be seen as a positive thing in lots of ways. People shared their cultures and were able to migrate. But for Africans, their story of migration took a dark, horrific course in the next few hundred years.

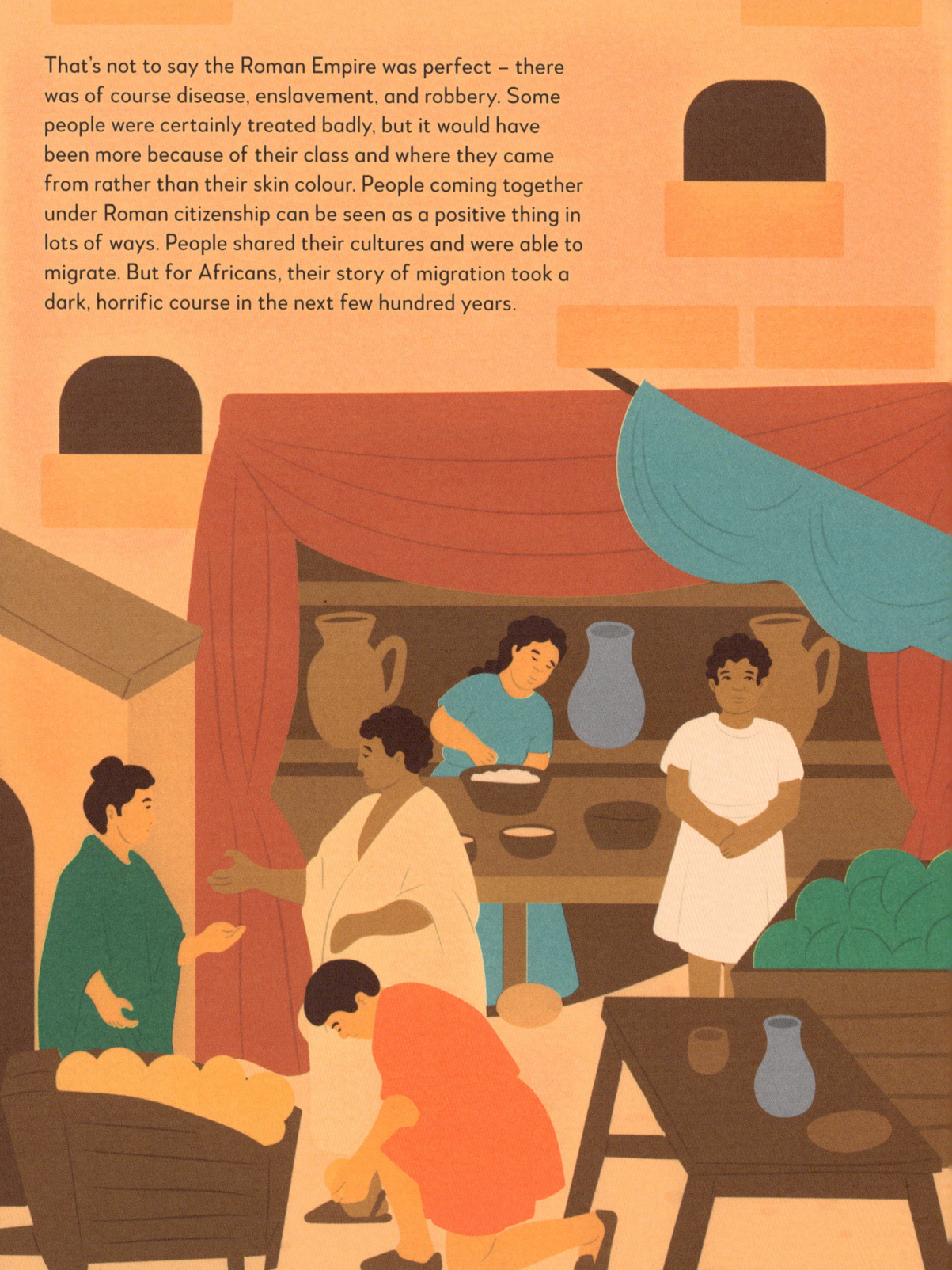

Britain's Black Tudors

African people lived in Britain during the Tudor period. They did all kinds of jobs within society. It is interesting to consider how Africans were treated in Britain during this time, particularly because generations that came after them faced enslavement. This chapter will also look at how Spain and Portugal played a big part in African migration to Britain.

African Migration During Tudor Times

African people were living in British society during the Tudor period, before the transatlantic enslavement of Africans. It wasn't uncommon for them to be living freely and working as servants, musicians, tailors, and at other trades.

Tailor (someone who makes or mends clothes)

Servant (someone who is paid to work in another person's home)

Parish records

Parish records from burials and marriages show that many Africans were living in Tudor England. The fact that they had Christian burials and weddings in the church shows that they were respected. Although there were differences in terms of appearance and heritage, Africans were accepted in society.

When they arrived in Britain, many Africans settled in Edinburgh in Scotland, Hull in the north of England, and Plymouth and Truro in the south west, as well as the larger cities of London, Southampton, and Bristol.

Who Was Sir Francis Drake,
and What Did He Have to do With African Migrants Coming to England?

Many African people came over to Britain with British merchants. They were employed as servants and lived in British households.

Sir Francis Drake was a naval officer, slave trader, and privateer, meaning someone who was asked by the government to raid enemy ships. England and Spain were rivals, and Drake went to Panama, Central America to raid Spanish treasure ships. While there, he met the Cimarron people. They were Africans who had escaped enslavement by the Spanish and formed a large, powerful community. They disliked the Spanish as much as Drake did, and they formed an alliance together against the Spanish.

Sir Francis Drake

Sir Francis Drake met the Cimarron people in Panama.

Sir Francis also met a young man called Diego. He had been enslaved by the Spanish and escaped. He acted as a guide and interpreter for Drake and connected him to the leader of the Cimarron people. Diego returned to England with Drake in 1573 and lived in his household in Plymouth for four years, before joining him on his around the world voyage. Diego was paid wages, and while his relationship with Drake wasn't equal, they both benefited from it. Some people who returned with the English saw it as a better alternative to being enslaved by the Spanish.

Some African people were captured by Drake and other sea captains, however. In 1586, Drake and his fleet returned from the Caribbean, having raided the Spanish there. They captured 150 African people who had been previously captured by the Spanish, and planned to take them to Plymouth, England. However, after a terrible storm many of the English and Africans on board his ship died. Only three Africans made it back to Plymouth. One of them ended up living in the household of Henry Percy, ninth Earl of Northumberland.

Sadly, some Africans were treated badly and even sold as enslaved people, even though this was illegal in Britain at this time. In 1566, a seaman named John Lax illegally sold an African man to Hector Nunes, a Portuguese doctor living in London. The man had been captured in a raid by Drake on the city of Santo Domingo in what is now the Dominican Republic.

Edward Swarthye

Another African man living in Britain at this time was Edward Swarthye. He was a porter to Sir Edward Wynter, who was a sea captain and Member of Parliament living in Lydney, Gloucestershire. Wynter captained the ship the *Aid* on one of Drake's voyages. In 1597, Swarthye arrived in England with Wynter.

How Did African People Benefit the Sea Captains?

Coming back to Britain with the sea captains was not always a free choice for African people. They were often exploited for the sea captains' benefit. The sea captains sometimes "gave" African people as a gift to those in power in exchange for financial support. This allowed the sea captains to continue to raid enemy ships abroad.

Ships would sail to places such as Panama in Central America.

For example, Paul Bayning, the Viscount of Sudbury in Suffolk, paid for expeditions in 1595 and 1598. At least five African people, including three women, were recorded to be living in his household. It is likely that the Africans were "gifted" to him in exchange for his continued financial support.

Gold

Perfumes

Ivory

Pepper

In December 1590, a ship docked in Barnstaple, a river port town in Devon. The ship had returned from the Guinea coast in West Africa with £16,000 worth of gold, perfumes, ivory, and pepper. A year later the crew brought more goods back from Guinea, worth £10,000. Parish records show that nine Africans were living in Barnstaple between 1596 and 1607.

African Migrants and the Royal Family

The royal courts were also known to have had African servants. When Catherine of Aragon, a Spanish princess, came to England to marry Henry VIII, she brought with her a group of Black assistants. Among them was her most trusted lady in waiting, Catalina de Cardones. Ladies in waiting traditionally had high status and were good friends to those they served.

When Catherine's daughter, Mary Tudor, married Phillip II of Spain, he also brought at least one Black servant with him to the English court.

Catalina de Cardones with Catherine of Aragon.

John Blanke and the Royal court

The staff Catherine of Aragon had brought most likely included John Blanke. He was a trumpeter who played at the royal procession in 1511 to celebrate the birth of Henry VIII's first son. Blanke famously asked the king for a pay rise when he discovered he wasn't getting paid as much as the other trumpeters – and the king gave it to him! Blanke clearly had the confidence to directly ask the king for more money, because he knew his worth. An illustration of John Blanke can be seen on the Westminster Tournament Roll, a 60-foot-long manuscript.

Jacques Francis and the *Mary Rose*

Jacques Francis was an experienced deep diver from the Guinea coast who arrived in Southampton in the 1540s. He had been living there for a few years before he was recruited to salvage the *Mary Rose*, Henry VIII's favourite warship that had sunk in 1545. Jacques Francis had to give evidence in court against his employer, Piero Paolo Corsi, an Italian who had been accused of theft from another salvage dive. Francis was the first African man allowed to stand up in court, as he was considered a free man in the eyes of the law.

What Other Roles Did African People Play When They Came to England?

English traders often brought African people back to England from Morocco, Guinea, and South Africa to be trained as interpreters and traders. The African people would then work for the English in their future business in these regions.

We can find evidence of this happening in 1555. English trader John Lok brought five men from the area now known as Ghana. Records of the time described the men as strong, and said that they enjoyed the food they ate but weren't keen on the cold climate. They stayed in Lok's household and learnt English.

Three of them returned to Ghana in 1556, much to the relief of their community. The other two men returned in 1562. In 1577, William Towerson, one of the traders who they had dealt with, met with the last two men again. They brought Towerson two pounds of gold, to encourage him to work with them again.

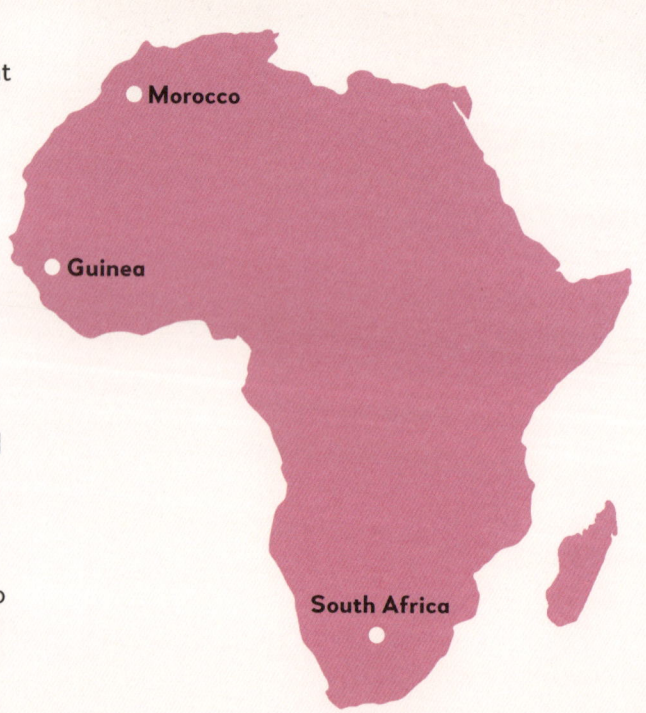

The men stayed in John Lok's
household, where they learnt
English, before returning to Ghana.

Let's not forget that the African men in this
story were being used unfairly to the English traders'
advantage. There are other examples of African people
being sold illegally as slaves, too. Stories like this are a
big reason why some African people came to Britain at
this time, so it is important to know about them.

Elizabeth I and African Migrants

African people had settled into English life. It was common for them to live in English people's houses and to be seen in the streets and the ports. They were poor, but part of society. However in the 1590s, Elizabeth I declared that harvests had failed and there was hunger and disease. She tried to place the blame for this bad situation on the African people living in England.

Many Africans living in England were of Muslim faith. Elizabeth I used this against them, labelling them non-believers of Christianity. She instructed merchant Casper van Senden to start deporting Africans, and set up a deal with Spain and Portugal to exchange them for English Catholic prisoners. Many people were angry about this. Those who had African servants didn't want to let them go. The irony was that even though Elizabeth I had tried to

Elizabeth I ruled from 1558-1603.

blame the Africans for the bad situation, she herself had an African maidservant called Mary Radcliffe. Despite the efforts of Elizabeth I, the numbers of Africans coming to England continued to rise between 1585 and 1604, the time of the Anglo-Spanish War.

Spain, Portugal, and North Africa

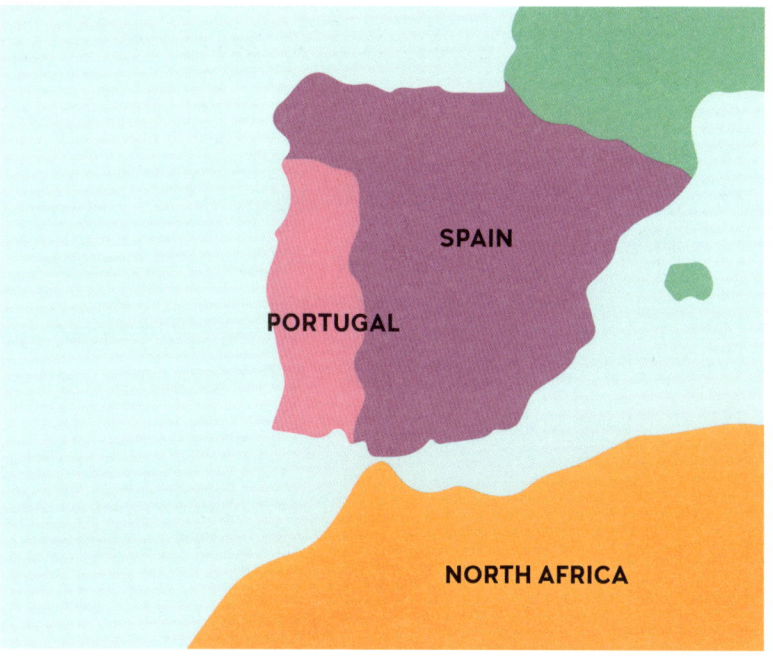

The English landscape was changing, and more Africans were arriving. Some arrived with their employer, some had been pressured into migrating for a short period, and some had been enslaved illegally. The number of African people coming to England was also increased by the conflict with Spain and Portugal. Enslaved African people worked on Spanish ships during the war, and many saw it as an opportunity to escape enslavement from the Spanish. They escaped and went back with the English in the hope of a better life.

Migration in the 18th and 19th Centuries

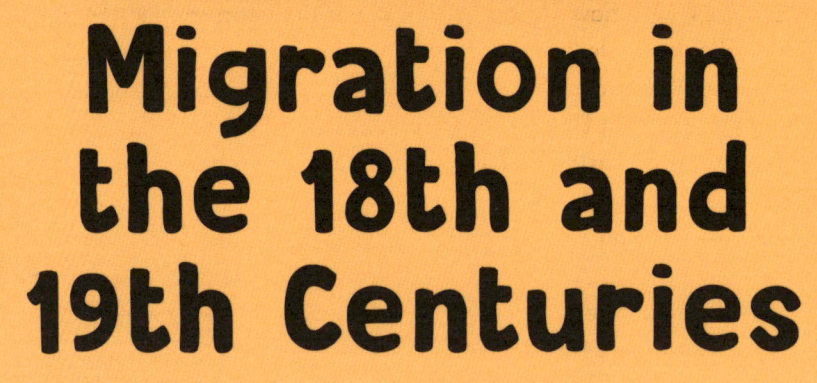

This chapter explores more how enslavement and Black people living in Britain were linked. We said in the introduction to this book that Black history is about more than enslavement, but we still need to understand the huge impact that enslavement had.

In this chapter, you may notice that we are slowly changing our language from talking about people of African and Caribbean descent to instead using the word Black.

Over the years, Black African and Caribbean people started identifying more as Black, because they were connected by their experience and how they were treated. People in Britain often only noticed their appearance, such as skin tone, not what country they were from. "Black" therefore became a political identity that allowed people of African and Caribbean descent to connect.

Why Was Living in Britain Very Difficult for Some Black People?

Throughout the mid-18th century, the Black population continued to grow steadily in Britain. People worked in various trades and as domestic servants. Many had also migrated from North America having escaped enslavement.

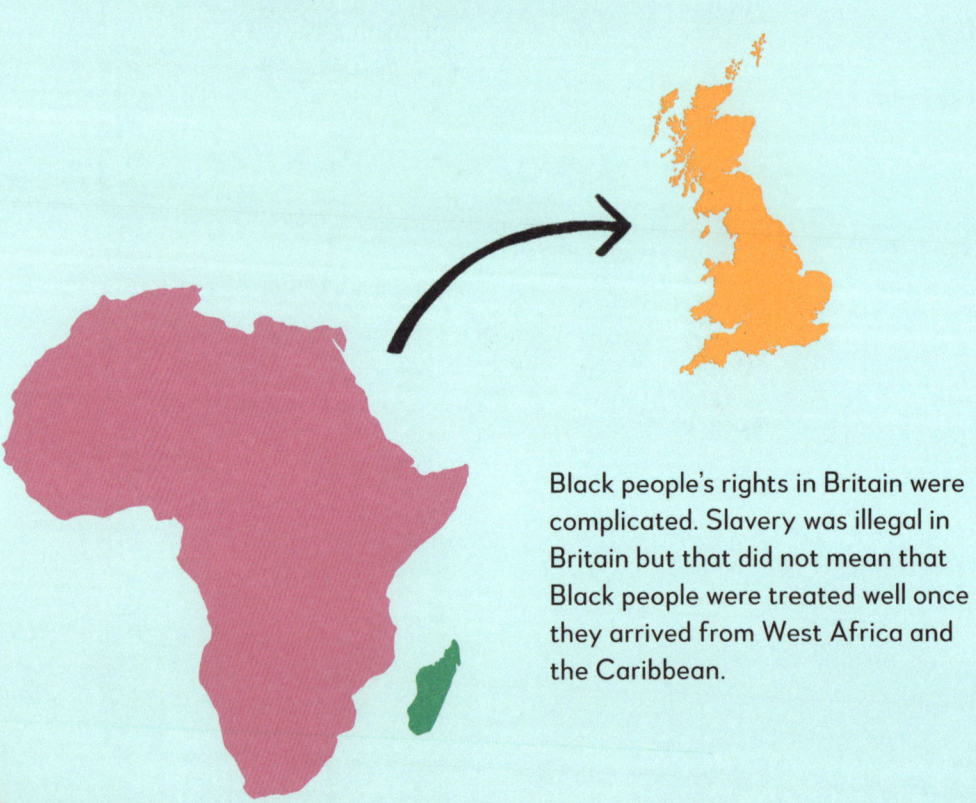

Black people's rights in Britain were complicated. Slavery was illegal in Britain but that did not mean that Black people were treated well once they arrived from West Africa and the Caribbean.

The Somerset case in 1772 had confirmed that slavery on English soil was not supported in law. But slavery was not abolished abroad until 1833.

The law was there to protect Africans, but people didn't always obey the law. Some servants were treated harshly, even though they were technically free according to British law.

There were many dreadful traders who, once they had returned from Africa selling and buying goods, took the chance to sell African people to British people in town and city ports such as Liverpool and Bristol.

Who Were Some Free Black People Who Lived in Britain?

Some Black people lived free and successful lives in Britain. In some cases, they had come as enslaved people and were later freed. But some came to Britain as free people. They worked as musicians, entrepreneurs, and secretaries.

To name a few, there was **Joseph Emidy**, a violinist who eventually became leader of the Truro Philharmonic Orchestra; **George Augustus Polgreen Bridgetower**, another violinist who was linked to Ludwig van Beethoven; **Cesar Picton**, a business owner who owned a wharf and malt house; **Dido Elizabeth Belle**, the daughter of the British naval officer Sir John Lindsay, who helped him run his legal affairs; and **George Africanus**, a business owner who created an employment agency called "Africanus' Register of Servants". They were all free individuals. Why not go online or to your local library and see what else you can find out about them?

Dido Elizabeth Belle

George Africanus

Who was Francis Barber?

Francis Barber was secretary to writer and poet Samuel Johnson. He helped Johnson adapt the first *Dictionary of the English Language*, which was published in 1755. Barber was born in enslavement in Jamaica in 1735 and was brought to England in 1750 by Colonel Richard Bathurst. He ended up working for Johnson, and they became good friends. Johnson was so fond of Barber that he paid for him to attend Bishop's Stortford School, a boarding school in Hertfordshire. When Johnson died in 1784, he left Barber a gold watch and retirement funds, which showed how important Barber was to him. A gold watch would have been worth a lot of money!

The case of James Somerset

The case of James Somerset in 1772 triggered the decline of the enslavement of Black people. A merchant called Charles Stewart had originally bought Somerset in Virginia, North America, before coming to England. After working for Stewart for two decades, Somerset escaped in November 1771 in London. He was recaptured two months later and was put on a ship heading to Jamaica. Granville Sharp, an anti-slavery campaigner, ensured that Somerset was given a trial. The Lord Chief Justice, Lord Mansfield, eventually ruled that since slavery was not lawful on British soil, no enslaved person could forcibly be removed from Britain and sold into slavery. This meant Somerset was a free man!

This was an important case that made people question why enslavement was allowed to continue in America, when it was not lawful in Britain. It is really important for us to understand that the ruling by Lord Mansfield didn't mean enslavement didn't still happen in Britain. It was illegal, but people were technically still living as enslaved people in some cases. It was also some years until the slave trade was finally outlawed.

The Black Loyalists

In 1775, the British were fighting the American War of Independence. The British had promised to free enslaved people who had escaped plantations, but only if they helped fight the war with them. The people who agreed were called "Black Loyalists", because they were loyal to the British.

After the British lost the American War of Independence, they returned home with 400 Black Loyalists in the 1780s. This itself can be seen as a mass migration of Black people. Once in Britain, many Black Loyalists found themselves in severe poverty.

The Loyalist Claims Commission was an organisation set up to support those who were extremely poor. Unfortunately, not everyone was able to access these funds. Less than 50 Loyalists out of 400 received the money that was supposed to support them. The fact that Black Loyalists were visibly living in poverty made a lot of people in Britain uncomfortable.

SIERRA LEONE

It was then decided that the Loyalists would be resettled in Sierra Leone on the west coast of Africa. Henry Smeathman was a naturalist (someone who studies plants, animals and insects). He was given the job of organising the resettlement process, having been to Sierra Leone previously to collect plant samples for Kew Gardens. However, he wasn't to be trusted.

Smeathman didn't really care about the Loyalists and only wanted to make money. He was planning to cultivate cotton and had the financial backing of two London merchants. He had sold the idea of Sierra Leone being the ideal home for the Loyalists to live, even though the weather was stormy and rough, and tropical diseases like malaria were deadly.

Cotton plant

Nova Scotia

Not all Black Loyalists were in favour of being resettled in Sierra Leone. We should remember that this group of people would have been moved around – by force – for most of their lives. Some had wanted to resettle in the Nova Scotia colony or the Caribbean. Some Black Loyalists had, in fact, stayed in Canada when the British returned home after the war.

The government came up with an incentive to encourage people to go to Sierra Leone. They would give the Loyalists a weekly allowance if they went to Sierra Leone. Loyalists who could read made sure that the plan of action the Commission had created would support them in the best way. The Treasury (the part of the government that controls public money) had agreed to pay £14 per person for three months of food, tools, clothes, and some building materials.

There was a lot of interest from the public about what was going on. As well as Black Loyalists, some Black domestic servants (who had already been living in London pre-1780), started to consider setting up a new life in Sierra Leone. Some couldn't see a future in Britain, so resettling to Sierra Leone seemed like a better option.

The journey from Deptford to Sierra Leone

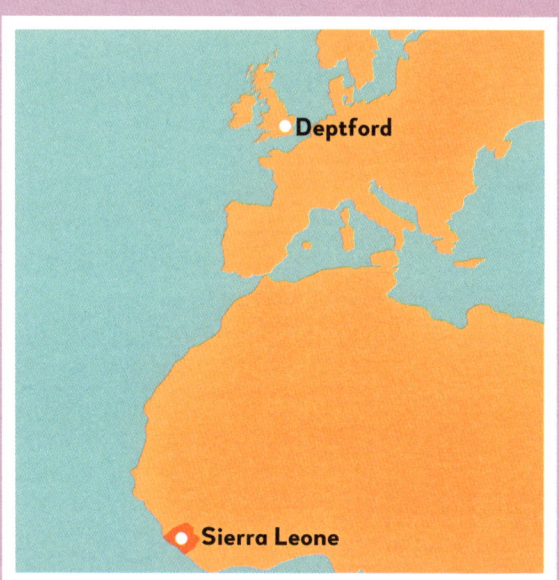

A fleet of three ships set sail from Deptford, London in April 1787. Unfortunately, the conditions for the new arrivals were dreadful. The heavy rains made it difficult to grow anything or build housing. Supplies from England soon ran out. Many people also died of diseases like malaria. However, the people stayed and made Sierra Leone their home.

The cultures of all the people who had gone to Sierra Leone blended together. They became known as the Krios people. The Krios people of Sierra Leone were made up of four different groups: Black people from Britain; Maroons from Jamaica; the Black Loyalists (including some who had come from Nova Scotia); and liberated Africans who were rescued while being transported to plantations in the Caribbean after slavery was abolished. Today, Krios culture remains strong in Sierra Leone. They have their own language, known as Krio, which is spoken by most people in Sierra Leone.

The Beginning of the Abolishment of Enslavement

Many formerly enslaved people spoke out about the abuse of their human rights. They spread the word of the true horrors of enslavement after being kidnapped from their homes thousands of miles away. Certain figures had a big impact in England when they started to campaign for the abolition of enslavement. It is important to learn about these figures when we learn about slavery, to get the full story.

Olaudah Equiano was taken from the Kingdom of Benin (now modern-day Nigeria in West Africa) when he was 11 years old. He was sold to a Royal Naval Officer called Michael Henry Pascal and spent his time aboard naval ships. He was baptised and taught English, which was rare for a former enslaved person in the 18th century. Equiano was eventually able to buy his freedom.

He became a member of the Sons of Africa who were considered Britain's first Black political group. They were made up of former slaves who wanted to be involved in the abolishment of enslavement. Equiano's friend Ottobah Cugoano was also a member. Originally from Ghana, Cugoano was enslaved in 1770 at 13 years old and was given his freedom in 1772.

OLAUDAH
EQUIANO

Equiano and Cugoano both wrote books about their experiences. Equiano's book was called *The Interesting Narrative of the Life of Olaudah Equiano*. It told of his experiences of being enslaved. The book was read by many people and helped to fuel the anti-slavery movement.

Enslavement was officially made illegal by Parliament in 1833 throughout the entire British Empire. Many Black people continued to migrate here from North America to escape the horrible treatment they had faced. Even though Britain had played a huge role in enslavement, many saw the nation as a safe place compared to the American Caribbean plantations.

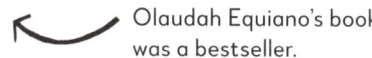 Olaudah Equiano's book was a bestseller.

Cugoano's book was called *Thoughts and Sentiments on the Evil and Wicked Traffic of the Slavery and Commerce of the Human Species*. It was read by many people, even the Royal Family. The Sons of Africa spent much of their time campaigning, writing memoirs and newspaper articles, and organising public speeches and petitions.

Today, there is a blue plaque commemorating Ottobah Cugoano at Schomberg House in London.

OTTOBAH
CUGOANO
born c.1757

Author and
anti-slavery campaigner

lived and worked in
Schomberg House
1784–1791

Public opinion about enslavement was starting to change. As formerly enslaved people like Equiano and Cugoano spoke out about their experiences, people were being made more aware of the injustices they faced. All the work they and the Sons of Africa did contributed to Parliament passing new acts to bring the end of enslavement.

A Mix of Black Migration

The mid-18th century was a key time when Black people migrated to Britain and other places in the world. Sometimes they had come as enslaved people, but the stories of Black people who were free individuals and came to Britain to work shouldn't be ignored. The Transatlantic Slave Trade affected millions of Black people, but there were a number of Black people who lived different lives, and it is important that we remember them when we talk about this period of history. We shouldn't only see Black people of this time as being the subjects of enslavement. There were many who carved their own path, including Black people who campaigned against slavery.

Black people came to Britain for all kinds of reasons, for example, the Black Loyalists.

Many Black people in Britain were free and earned a living.

People like Olaudah Equiano, who campaigned for the end of slavery, changed history.

Edmonia Lewis

We have read about enslavement and the end of enslavement in this chapter. It is also important to hear about how some people came to Britain for different reasons.

Edmonia Lewis was a celebrated individual with a remarkable migration journey. She was born a free woman in America in 1844 and became a sculptor. She left to travel to Italy, and eventually settled in London in 1901. Lewis sold one of her sculptures to pay for her journey. She left America as she felt that she couldn't work freely as a Black artist where she was constantly reminded of her colour.

She was the first Black American sculptor that we know of. Her work represented Black people in the Neoclassical style popular in the late 19th century.

Even though her final years were lived quietly in London, it is inspiring to know that Lewis followed her dreams and left America freely to become a famous sculptor. What else can you find out about Edmonia Lewis, and what were some of her famous works? Which other Black figures migrated to Britain and found greatness during and after the time of abolishment of enslavement?

Edmonia Lewis made sculptures in a Neoclassical style.

Migration and the "Mother Country"

Profession: *Nurse*

Place of Birth: *Barbados*
Date of Birth: *4th September 19__*
Residence: *Barbados*
Height: *5'4*
Colour of Eyes: *Dark Brown*
Colour of Hair: *Brown*
Children / Dependants: *2*

Signature: *R. Johnson*

Photograph

UNITED KINGDOM OF GREAT BRITAIN AND NORTHERN IRELAND

EMPIR

LO

The ship *Empire Windrush* docked at Tilbury Docks in Essex on 22 June 1948. It is a famous example of migration from the Caribbean to Britain. In this chapter, we will look at the 20th century, and consider how Britain encouraged Commonwealth nationals to leave their countries to start a new life. We'll look at the ways the British government used imperialism to encourage people to rebuild Britain after World War II.

WINDRUSH

DON

Passenger Opportunity To
United Kingdom

POST

Dear Family,
I am delighted to
inform you that we
have arrived safely.
The weather is
cold...

CARD

2p
POSTAGE

Mrs Johnson
31 Hastings Road
Rivers Palace
Kingston
Jamaica

EMPIRE WINDRUSH

Commonwealth Citizens and the World Wars

German bombing from World War II had devastated parts of Britain, in particular London. It needed rebuilding and redeveloping quickly to get the economy back to normal. World Wars I and II weren't just fought by British men and women. Members of the Commonwealth nations were also called upon to join forces and fight in both World Wars. In World War II, a total of 15 million serving men and women were involved – that's a lot of people!

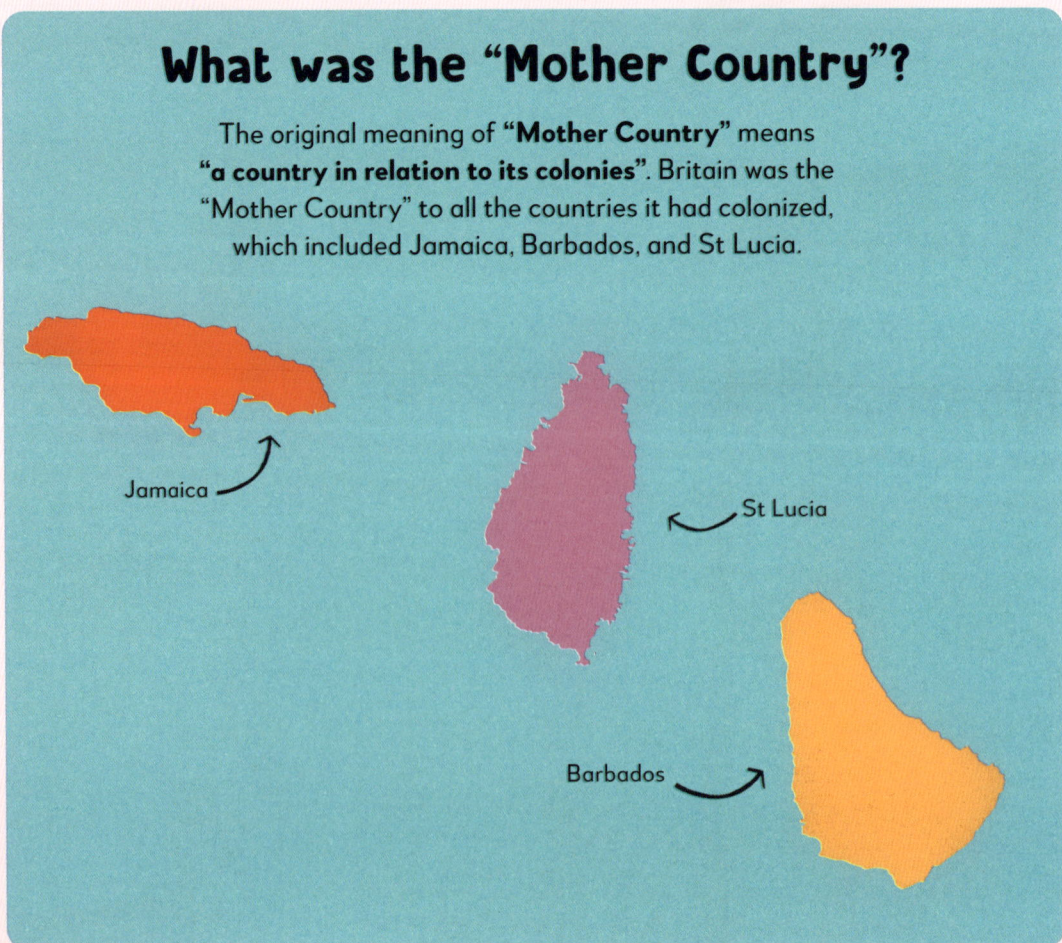

What was the "Mother Country"?

The original meaning of **"Mother Country"** means **"a country in relation to its colonies"**. Britain was the "Mother Country" to all the countries it had colonized, which included Jamaica, Barbados, and St Lucia.

Jamaica

St Lucia

Barbados

Britain was seen as very important in the lives of the Commonwealth citizens. Films and news bulletins would inform people of the events happening in Britain. The education children received was focused on the British way of life. They would sing the national anthem every morning and the Queen's face was on all the exercise books.

This way of making sure British culture was part of life in colonies is known as imperialism.

Children grew up with a strong sense that they truly belonged to the "Mother Country".

The Royal Family and the Commonwealth

The impact the Royal Family had on Caribbean society was significant. People waited until 4am to hear about Queen Elizabeth II's coronation on the radio, and newspapers reported the coronation on their front pages.

Britain wanted their colonial subjects to be involved and also to feel that being British was a big part of their identity.

People listened to the news of the Queen's coronation on the radio.

Protecting Queen and country

About 10,000 people from the Caribbean
fought alongside Britain in World War II.

Commonwealth citizens played a significant part in the World Wars.
During the wars, they were encouraged to protect the "Mother
Country". After World War II, Britain wanted to recruit people from
the colonies to fill jobs and help rebuild the country. Many of the
people who had fought as soldiers didn't hesitate to go to Britain
to help. They wanted to support it getting back on its feet.

How Did Commonwealth Citizens Get Jobs in Britain?

After the war, transport, healthcare, and hospitality needed strengthening in Britain. Various schemes were set up to recruit people to work in these jobs. Recruitment of Scottish, Welsh, and Irish nationals wasn't enough – more people were needed.

In 1956, London Transport (now known as Transport for London) set up recruitment schemes in Bridgetown, Barbados, and in Jamaica. They advertised in newspapers and on the radio, and word soon spread of new job opportunities in Britain.

THE SPACIOUS COMFORTABLE LUXURIOUS

Santa Maria

SAILS **AUGUST 26**th

via VIGO SPAIN

BOOK NOW FOR **ENGLAND**

KINGSTON TO LONDON FOR ONLY

£75

SEE YOUR TRAVEL AGENT IMMEDIATELY!

H. MACAULAY ORRETT LTD, 507 KING ST. KINGSTON

An advert for a ship sailing from Jamaica to London in the 1950s.

Nona Roberts was a bus conductor who was recruited from the Caribbean.

Participants had to complete an interview, a written test, and have a medical check-up. British Rail was also advertising in Barbados. The potential job roles were mainly geared towards men, however women were also recruited for bus conductor, station staff, and canteen roles. In 1966, the same recruitment drive for London Transport was set up in Trinidad.

Why Were Commonwealth Citizens So Important to the NHS?

The National Health Service (NHS) was established in 1948. It recruited men and women from the Caribbean to Britain to train as health workers.

Even Enoch Powell, who was the Minister of Health in 1960-63, and had openly racist views about Black people, was in favour of the campaign, so clearly there was a need for workers in Britain.

Britain relied on foreign nationals to keep the NHS running smoothly, just like it does today. One benefit for Commonwealth citizens was that the NHS and London Transport paid people's fares to Britain, and citizens would pay it back over two years.

Constance Nelson and Monica Munroe were two of the first Black nurses to work in the NHS.

In some cases, only single men were allowed to apply for certain positions. If you think back to the first chapter of this book, this is a stark difference to Roman migration, when a soldier's whole family would join him and set up home in their new country.

It was a struggle for single mothers. They would have left their children behind until they were settled enough for their children to join them in Britain.

Applicants had to go through an interview process.

Why Else Did Caribbean Citizens Leave for Britain?

We've talked about how lots of people from the Caribbean left their sunny climates to live in Britain because of their loyalty towards the "Mother Country" and wanting to be physically closer to it. However, this was not the only reason people migrated to Britain. Many people saw leaving the Islands as an opportunity to improve their lives.

Oppression by society, poverty, and escaping difficult family life were some other reasons for migrating. Many citizens wanted to take advantage of learning new skills – knowledge is power after all. People wanted to earn more money for themselves and their families, and many sent money back home on a regular basis. **What stories or accounts can you find of what made people decide to leave for Britain?**

Migration to old Commonwealth countries

Let's not forget that migration is something that is always happening. We must remember that many white British nationals also undertook a journey of migration between mid-1945 and 1946. These British nationals migrated to Australia, New Zealand, and Canada, because of labour shortages in these countries. Because of this, the British working population went down by 1.38 million people.

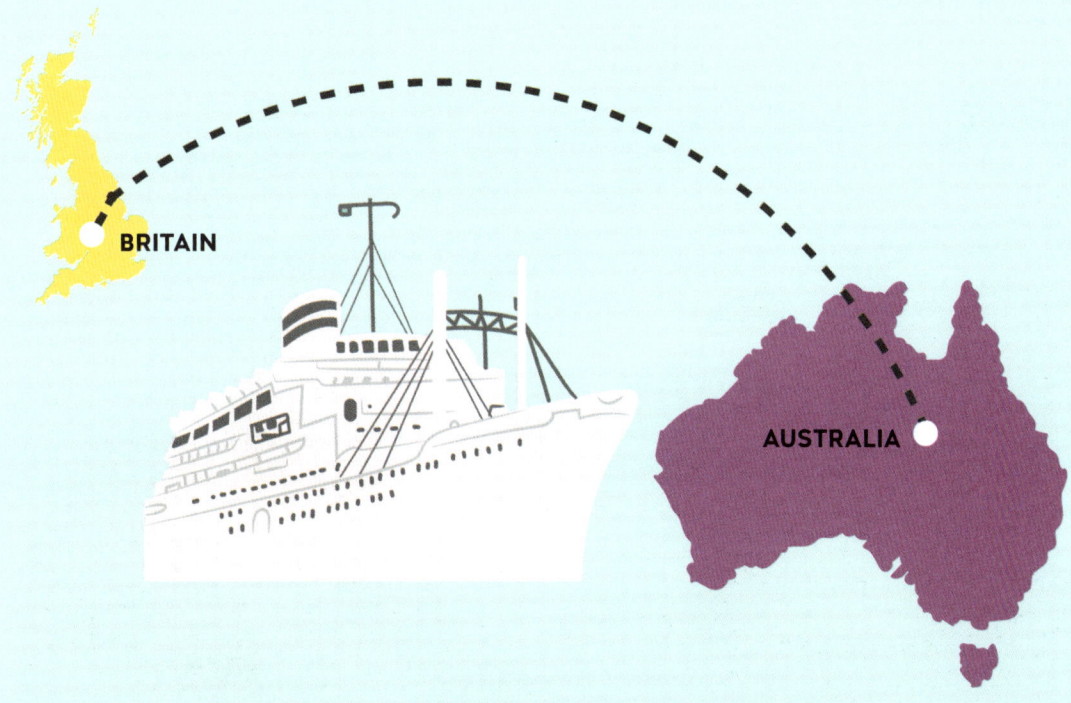

It is important to say here that, although these are both examples of migration, the reasons behind why Black and white people migrated were not the same. Black people left their countries because the legacy of enslavement and colonisation meant they had fewer opportunities in their countries.

White migrants were encouraged by the state to migrate to old Commonwealth countries where indigenous people had previously had their land taken from them during British colonial expansion. Although both are examples of migration, the contexts are different.

Was the Idea of the "Mother Country" a Myth?

Migrants may already have been expecting the cold, dark, greyness that Britain offered. Information about what to expect was given out before they left, and of course they would have heard all about the uninspiring climate from people who had already been to Britain!

People came to Britain with hope for the future.

What many migrants might not have expected were the structural inequalities and discriminatory attitudes that awaited them. This was very different from what they had been taught at school; the idea that the Commonwealth was one big, connected family. It wouldn't have been surprising if some had come to the conclusion that the "Mother Country" was a myth. The streets that were supposed to be paved with gold were dark, grey, and wet – not the new life they had hoped for.

A home away from home

People found support in their communities.

While many Black migrants faced racism, poverty, and hardship, they stayed strong and kept on going. Some people felt they couldn't go back home for fear of being shamed and berated for wasting an opportunity. They got jobs and they carried on building a new life. Having a community around to support each other helped. They enjoyed social activities and music, and while they might have had to tone down their colourful fashion and sunshine-filled music, they integrated into British society as best as they could and made it their home.

The Bronze Woman Statue in Stockwell Memorial Gardens, London shows a woman holding a child up to the sky. The statue represents the challenges the Black community, particularly Black women, faced when they migrated to Britain. It also represents hope and optimism for the future.

IN CONCLUSION...

The intention of this book is to understand that there are **many ways** that African people came to live and settle in Britain. There is more to the story of the migration of African people than the **transatlantic enslavement of Africans and post-war migration**. However, we **can't ignore** the **massive impact** these events had on how the world views **African people**.

That is why it is **SO important** to discover the many other **journeys Black people made** to Britain and other parts of the world! It is vital that those migration stories are **spoken** and **SHOUTED** about and that people **know about** the Black people who carved out **their own path in life of their own free will.**

Glossary

Throughout the book, you may have come across some words you don't know. Check here to find out all the meanings and learn something new! If you are struggling to understand any of the meanings, discuss them with a friend, a parent, a teacher, or someone you know.

Abolishment
Put an end to something, such as an organisation, rule, or custom.

Colonialism
Colonialism occurs when a country or a nation takes control of other nations, lands, regions, or territories outside of its own borders by turning those other nations, lands, regions, or territories into colonies.

Commonwealth
A group of 56 countries that includes the UK and independent nations that were once colonies within the British Empire. The countries have no legal obligations to one another but do cooperate on economic and humanitarian matters.

Imperialism
Imperialism is the idea of expanding one's territory by taking over another country. This is done by creating colonies or areas that have been taken over.

Indigenous
This word is used to describe people who originally lived in a particular place, rather than people who moved there later.

Industrialisation
Industrialisation is the process by which an economy is transformed from a primarily agricultural one to one based on the manufacturing of goods.

Migration
Migration is the movement of people from one area to another.

Mother Country
An imperial power in relation to its colonies.

Neoclassicism
Neoclassicism is the name given to an art movement that draws upon Western classical art and culture (usually that of ancient Greece or ancient Rome).

Privateer
Someone who is asked by the government to raid enemy ships.

Race
Race is just one category that people divide each other into. This might be based on appearance or where someone's ancestors are from. These categories have not always existed throughout history, but are something that society has invented over time.

Transatlantic enslavement of Africans
This was the slave trade involving the transportation by slave traders of various enslaved African people, mainly to the Americas.

You might also notice that we capitalise the B in Black, but not the w in white. Here is the Black Curriculum's note explaining why this is:

We capitalise the B in Black because the word Black in this context reflects a shared sense of identity and, to a certain extent, a community. The case for capitalising Black is also rooted in humanising and uplifting groups that have historically been stripped of this right. White, in this context, does not suffer from the same historical happenings, especially in the context of Britain.

In this book we have focused on Black British history; that's Black history from England, Wales, and Scotland. This is why you'll notice us talking about Britain, which is made up of England, Wales, and Scotland.

We're not referring to the UK, which is made up of Britain and Northern Ireland. Northern Ireland itself has so much Black history that we'd need a whole separate book to cover it properly.

Please note, the maps in this book are not to scale.

Index

THE BLACK CURRICULUM

Want to find out more about Black British history? Go to www.theblackcurriculum.com to find videos, zines, classroom resources, and more.

If you've enjoyed this book, look
out for the other books in this series!
Legacies: Black British Pioneers
and *Places: Important Sites
in Black British History.*

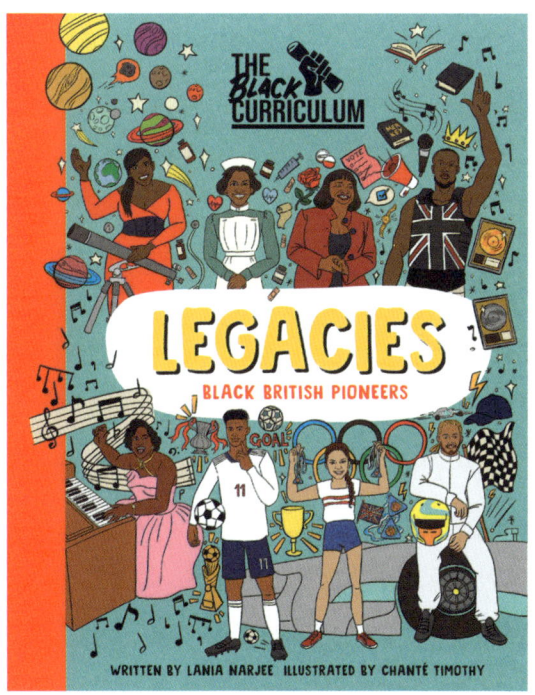

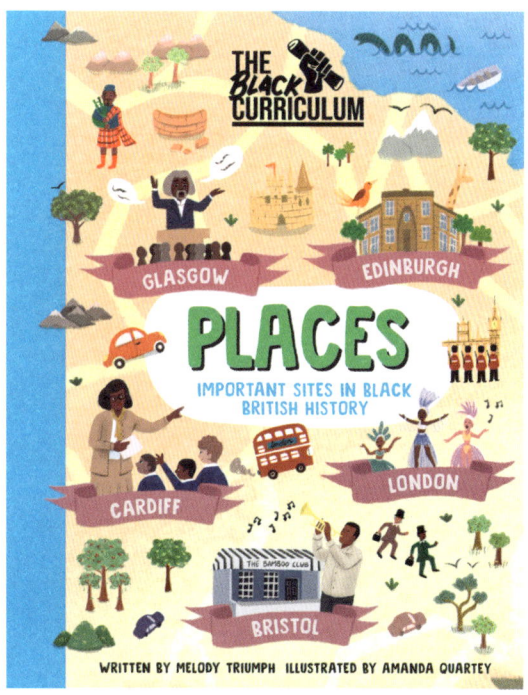

**Legacies:
Black British Pioneers**

Foreword by Lewis Hamilton

Written by Lania Narjee
Illustrated by Chanté Timothy

**Places: Important Sites
in Black British History**

Foreword by Darcus Beese

Written by Melody Triumph
Illustrated by Amanda Quartey

Project Editor Rosie Peet
Project Art Editor Stefan Georgiou
Senior Acquisitions Editor Katy Flint
Managing Art Editor Vicky Short
Production Editor Siu Yin Chan
Production Controller Louise Minihane
Publishing Director Mark Searle

Written by Millie Mensah
Illustrated by Camilla Ru

First published in Great Britain in
2022 by Dorling Kindersley Limited
DK, One Embassy Gardens, 8 Viaduct
Gardens, London SW11 7BW

The authorised representative in the EEA
is Dorling Kindersley Verlag GmbH. Arnulfstr.
124, 80636 Munich, Germany

Page design copyright © 2022 Dorling
Kindersley Limited
A Penguin Random House Company

Artwork copyright © Camilla Ru, 2022

Text copyright © The Black Curriculum CIC 2022

10 9 8 7 6 5 4 3 2
002–328146–Aug/2022

A CIP catalogue record for this book
is available from the British Library.
ISBN: 978-0-2415-5280-3

Printed in the UK

The publisher would like to thank Chima Itabor
for providing the authenticity read; Pamela
Afram, Victoria Armstrong, Lisa Gillespie,
and Julia March at DK for editorial support;
and Ilhan Rayen Awed and Saffa Khalil at
The Black Curriculum.

For the curious

www.dk.com

MIX
Paper | Supporting
responsible forestry
FSC™ C018179